MILDRED & KINGSLEY OKONKWO

NO DRY SEASON

A Devotional on Financial Prosperity for Couples

NO DRY SEASON

A Devotional On Financial Prosperity For Couples

ISBN 9798377746447

Published and Printed in Nigeria by:
MillionValues Concepts,
105, Igi-Olugbin, Pedro Road, Lagos
Tel: 08185710897 | millionvalues@gmail.com

To contact the author:
Tel: 08077714411, 08077714413

CONTENTS

INTRODUCTION

The Bible talks about the power of agreement, it says, ***When two of you get together on anything at all on earth and make a prayer of it, my Father in heaven goes into action [matthew 18:19]*** and we believe that more than anything the agreement a couple has as husband and wife is one of the most powerful forces. This is why satan constantly and consistently attacks that agreement.

Over the years, we have discovered that one of the areas the devil fights a couple the most is in the area of their finances. The reason for this is glaring; great ideas and dreams are frustrated when there is no money to bring them to reality. This can cause unnecessary tension in a marriage. Like we always say, as powerful as faith is, children don't eat faith and as beautiful as love is unfortunately, it doesn't pay the bills. You still need money because money answers all things.

A recent survey of 191 CDFA professionals from across North America showed the three leading causes of divorce were "basic incompatibility" (43%), "infidelity" (28%), and "money issues" (22%). And this cuts across irrespective of race, tribe, religion or years of marriage.

Let's be honest, our marriage is more beautiful with financial stability. We can plan exotic surprises for each other and appreciate each other better. However, it wasn't always this way. Things changed as a result of walking with God regarding our finances and standing on His Word, obeying the principles found in the word. Walking with God regarding our finances was non-negotiable because sometimes beyond our personal needs we were also involved in ministry projects that cost us millions of dollars.

How did things change? We looked through the scriptures, listened to messages, got out financial principles from God's word and started acting on them consistently. We knew it was God's will for us to enjoy prosperity like He said in His word, *"...Let the Lord be magnified who has* ***pleasure in the prosperity*** *of His servant" (Psalm 35:27 NKJV).* And this includes you and your spouse.

We saw God literally lift us from not having enough to having more than enough and now to a realm of generational wealth. It's our desire to walk through these same principles with you so that you too can move into financial freedom. We know that when more couples walk in prosperity, it becomes easy to influence our generation and expand God's kingdom here on earth. We pray that you will not only find this devotional helpful but that it will inspire you to find more of God's promises that can totally transform your life like it did ours .

Blessings,

Mildred and Kingsley Okonkwo

As powerful as faith is, Children don't eat faith and as beautiful as love is, it doesn't pay bills. You still need money because money answers all things.

DAY ONE

360-Degree Prosperity

Beloved, I pray that you may prosper in all things and be in health, just as your soul prospers.

—3 John 1:2 [KJV]

God designed your marriage to be prosperous. Amazingly, in more ways than you want it to prosper- in everything! No wonder the book of Ecclesiastes 4:9(NKJV) says, "Two *are* better than one, Because they have a good reward for their labour." Good reward here indicates that their union is prosperous.

Like Job, God wants you and your spouse to enjoy prosperity in ***all things.*** Job was the wealthiest and most respected man in the East (Job 1:3 AMP); he had sons and daughters, his sons threw parties regularly and had their sisters in attendance. This means they were obviously happy, healthy and with no worries. It also means they were living in peace and harmony as a family. They prospered spiritually, emotionally, financially, mentally, in every way.

The tenth verse of the message translation says of Job,

"You pamper him like a pet, make sure nothing bad ever happens to him or his family or his possessions, bless everything he does – he can't lose!"

Nothing screams 360-degree prosperity louder than this; everything is in order such that you have absolutely nothing to worry about. Money… check. Spiritual health… check. Physical health… check. Mental health… check. This is God's desire for you and your spouse. That you enjoy all-round prosperity.

SAY THIS TOGETHER

We declare that all-round prosperity is our reality. We prosper financially, we prosper physically, and we prosper mentally. In our emotions, we prosper. We are not triggered into making wrong choices. In our intellect, we prosper. We deal with issues with utmost intelligence. In our will, we prosper. We do not make moves and decisions outside the will of God. Our properties are protected, our children are healthy, and our minds are sound in Jesus name. Amen.

FURTHER STUDY:

Job 1: 1-5 (MSG)

DAY TWO

Keep Sowing

Then Isaac sowed in that land, and reaped in the same year a hundredfold, and the Lord blessed him. The man began to prosper, and continued prospering until he became very prosperous;

—Genesis 26:12-13 [NKJV]

In recent times, many families are migrating in search of greener pastures. I'm sure you've encountered this, at least we have, especially here in Nigeria where we are from. Everyone seems to be looking for ways to leave the country because they feel a certain level of despondency especially concerning their finances. This has also resulted in a lot of strain on marriages as partners are sometimes forced to live apart because they've had to abandon places known for their unfriendliness to businesses and stiff circulation of money for places that seemingly *'flow with milk and honey'*.

This would seem a logical move to make, who doesn't want to be in a land where everything works? However, faith and the promises of God trump logic any day so we must be careful not to move solely on logic.

Isaac was literally living in the "enemies camp"; a land where they envied him and tried to make it impossible for him to prosper. He ordinarily should not have survived let alone thrived, but God was with him.

Here are two things we can learn as a couple from Isaac:

1. He stood on God's promises. *Genesis 26: 2-4.*

   As a couple, walk in the consciousness of God's promises to you regarding wealth and riches. Search them out and meditate on them until they are ingrained in your heart. His promises are not subject to geographical location or any other external forces.

2. He sowed. *Genesis 26:12.*

Sowing is non-negotiable. It is one of the ways you plug into God's abundance. Plan together to give regularly towards God's work. Don't overlook paying your tithes, offerings and other faith seeds - they open up the windows of heaven over your home and keep the devourer away - (Malachi 3:10).

SAY THIS TOGETHER

We prosper regardless of where we are located. Everything we put our hands to do succeeds. We prosper on every side because we are children of the Promise. We declare that the seas favour us, the airways favour us, and the earth favours us. We declare that riches, honour and a satisfying life are ours in Jesus name. Amen.

FURTHER STUDY

Mark 4:20 (NLT)

DAY THREE

Submit to God

"Submit to God and be at peace with Him; In this way prosperity will come to you.

—Job 22:21 [NIV]

Have you ever been to an event or party where you are close friends with the host? If you have, then you know the perks of being the host's special guest. It would be in your interest to sit where the host asks you to sit because that's a guarantee that all the goodies that go around will definitely come to you, possibly before others. He hired the caterers and the waiters; he tells them where to go and what to do. It would be unwise not to follow the lead of such a person as far as that event is concerned.

A lot of couples sideline God when it comes to their finances. Much like the person who attends a party and ignores the host. They think they know what would work best. They have looked at the stock market and studied the statistics and economic implications and so they run off making what they think are smart decisions thereby sidelining the One who gives them the wisdom and power to get wealth.

In the scripture focus for today, Isaac's original plan was to run to Egypt during the famine, but God told him not to go to Egypt. He was to remain with the Amalekites and that was where he prospered greatly (Genesis 26). Interestingly many couples have a plan; sometimes the plan has even worked for them for a couple of years then something changes. Truth is only God knows the end from the beginning and he's in charge of times and seasons. So trusting Him is the best thing for you. Running to Egypt may have been a good idea from a natural viewpoint but Isaac would have missed it completely if he didn't trust God to run his life. God is the host running the event of our lives including our finances, why don't you let Him tell you where to sit?

SAY THIS TOGETHER

We surrender to God's sovereignty. We do not lean on our own understanding for anything because we only know in part. We submit our will and desires to the One who sees the hearts and motives of men. No matter how badly we think we want it, we declare God has the final say. We submit our businesses, careers, and financial plans to the One who knows the end from the beginning. We receive direction and we know what to do at all times.

FURTHER STUDY

Psalm 34:9-10 (NLT), Proverbs 5: 3-5 (NLT)

DAY FOUR

Financial Freedom

The Lord will open his storehouse where he keeps his rich blessings. He will send rain at the right time for your land. He will bless everything you do. You will have money to lend to many nations. And you will not need to borrow anything from them.

—Deuteronomy 28:12 [NIV]

There is nothing more beautiful than financial freedom. A realm where all your needs are supplied in abundance and money no longer determines what you can or cannot buy. A realm where you lend and don't borrow, where you are self-sufficient in God no matter the need. Even the thought of it is beautiful.

I once heard my pastor narrate an encounter he had with God. God had asked him a question, "Which is better: begging, borrowing or believing?" And, for a second, he was confused because they all yield the same result; they enable you to have your request. In fact, begging and borrowing in some cases give faster results than believing. After thinking about it for a while, he realised that believing was better because it gave multiple results, without degrading you or causing shame and fear and gives a heart overflowing with joy in God's ability to provide.

People borrow for different reasons, but whatever the reason is, no matter how crucial the need to borrow, a debtor remains a slave to their creditors until all debts are paid. The challenge with borrowing is this, like gambling and other drugs, it provides temporary relief to a much deeper issue. This is the reason it has the tendency to become addictive. The solution is to avoid borrowing or owing as much as you can and aim to eradicate it completely eventually.

God's word says, "He will send rain ***at the right time*** *for your land."* Yes, life happens and emergencies could come up that require you to respond with much urgency, but

God promises His children a 'right-on-time' provision, which means you will never be stranded. When the disciples needed to pay taxes Jesus instructed them in *Matthew 17:27[MSG], "...go down to the lake, cast a hook, and pull in the first fish that bites. Open its mouth and you'll find a coin. Take it and give it to the tax men. It will be enough for both of us."*

I can't count how many times God has shown up right on time when it comes to paying bills in our family. One thing I know is that with God, you can never be stranded financially. NEVER!!!

SAY THIS TOGETHER

We declare that in this family, we are lenders and not borrowers. The heavens are open unto us. Our source is not our business, salary or even a trust fund. We acknowledge God as our source therefore our supply comes from Him. When there is famine, we dwell in abundance because we operate with wisdom from above for saving and investing. We lend to nations and will never need to borrow. Every outstanding debt is cleared in Jesus' name. Amen.

FURTHER STUDY

Deuteronomy 11:14 (NIV), Leviticus 26:4 (NLT)

DAY FIVE

God Has a Plan

I know what I'm doing. I have it all planned out—plans to take care of you, not abandon you, plans to give you the future you hope for.

—Jeremiah 29:11 [MSG]

We've been married for some time now and sometimes when we look back at how we started, very broke by the way, we cannot help but acknowledge that God truly is a master planner. When we look at how much He's blessed us and the ways He has used to bless us, we know it's not random; it's very clear that He had a plan and simply moved us through that plan.

Now, you think back. Has God ever come through for you in a way you could never have anticipated? If yes, then why are you suddenly frantic about your financial situation? Relax, God is in control. Stop trying to figure out what He is doing, you can't. Simply bask in His promise that He has it all planned out, and trust me, those plans don't include leaving you stranded or desolate. He has a great plan to take care of you and He will. Maybe the reason you might be feeling helpless is that you are looking to something or someone else to come to your aid and rescue you instead of God.

Maybe your own concern is for the future; your children and what you will leave behind for them as an inheritance given the situation of the economy globally. Well, stop that right now. Stop worrying. In fact, be careful so that your worries don't start to affect your hope. This may be a good time to take your mind off the news, instead spend time in the good news; allow the Word of God (His Promises) to dwell in you richly. Declare God's promises over your home together. God knows what He is doing. Relax.

SAY THIS TOGETHER

We declare in the name of Jesus that we rest in the knowledge of God's goodness. That our hearts are always in tune with the Lord's. We do not worry about our finances or our future because we know Whom we have trusted. Our children prosper and they prosper for good. Our businesses and careers prosper and they prosper for good. We will not be moved by the world's system. We live above it with the confidence that You know what You are doing; You have it all planned out so we receive a future better than the one we hope for in Jesus name. Amen.

FURTHER STUDY

1 Kings 2:3 (NASB), Joshua 1:8 (BSB), Philippians 4:8 (NLT).

DAY SIX

Follow God's Instructions

They are like trees planted along the riverbank, bearing fruit each season. Their leaves never wither, and they prosper in all they do.

—Psalm 1:3 [NLT]

The pandemic and lockdown in 2020 as a result of COVID-19 saw the wrecking of a lot of businesses. The depression rate among entrepreneurs skyrocketed. People lost their jobs because companies could no longer retain them. It was a bad year for a lot of people financially. But in that same year, when others cried that there was a casting down, many others who were planted in God and saw Him as their Source celebrated a lifting.

The year 2020, was a good year for us. No, let me rephrase that, 2020 was a great year for us. We prospered like never before; from multiple streams of income to global relevance. I still remember how scared people were when the whole world literally shut down and it seemed like there was no way to earn a living. Naturally speaking it seemed like all channels of income were closed but interestingly in the midst of that, God still caused us to bear fruit in that season and our leaves did not wither. We were fruitful during the pandemic.

One of our major secrets was following God's instructions. He told us what platforms to get on, He opened our eyes to things that were valuable that we had access to but never paid attention to before. He opened our eyes to possibilities all around us and things literally turned around. I'm sure He's trying to get the same information across to you. Ask yourselves, as a couple, what has God asked you and your spouse to do? Now get to it! It will change your life and finances.

SAY THIS TOGETHER

We declare that we are divinely positioned for prosperity because we hear the voice of the Holy Spirit, and we follow His lead for every business and financial decision we make. Our hearts are yielded to God. We receive International recognition, we are invited to global platforms, and we earn in foreign currencies because the hand of the Lord is upon us. We enjoy fellowship with Him and we hear His will for us in Jesus name. Amen.

FURTHER STUDY

Psalm 92:14 (CSB), Jeremiah 17:8 (CEV).

DAY SEVEN

Secret Treasures

I will give you hidden treasures, riches stored in secret places, so that you may know that I am the LORD, the God of Israel, who summons you by name.

—Isaiah 45:3 [NIV]

I'm a shopper. I'm not even going to lie. I love shopping, especially for kids. I don't think I will ever be one of those people that will go on a vacation, and like my husband, head to the beaches, spend a day at the pool, go hiking and then come home and say they had a great time. If truth be told you will probably find me in a mall or on the high streets searching for secret treasures in unknown stores.

Now, as I said, some of the fondest times for me are when I walk into a shop that looks like it should actually be closed down (and this has happened a couple of times) and I suggest to people who go shopping with me that we should enter a shop, their response is usually, "Pastor M! What do you expect to find there?" Well, let's just say after they enter the store with me that one time they never ask me that again. I always find what I literally classify as treasures; amazing things at unbelievable prices hidden, maybe one or two things lying around somewhere looking unassuming.

See, even with something as basic as shopping, I shop confidently because I know that I am bound to find some secret treasure. I know that I will find something that's not hidden ***from*** me but ***for*** me. That's how walking with God concerning your finances can be. If you follow Him like others follow me when I want to go shopping, He will show you secret riches. Spend time with Him and let Him lead you and show you treasures He has hidden for both of you.

SAY THIS TOGETHER

We declare that our eyes are open to hidden riches. Business ideas that have not yet been explored are revealed unto us, fresh innovations that will wow the world come to us. God takes us to the places He has kept these hidden riches; He calls us by name, He reveals them to us because they are hidden for us and not from us in Jesus name. Amen.

FURTHER STUDY

Job 21:11 (GWT)

DAY EIGHT

Never Stranded

I will always show you where to go. I'll give you a full life in the emptiest of places— firm muscles, strong bones. You'll be like a well-watered garden, a gurgling spring that never runs dry.

—Isaiah 58:11 [MSG]

One of the biggest fears we have as human beings is the fear of uncertainty. Falling in love, dating, getting married is all well and good till you actually now get home from the honeymoon and it hits you that you don't really know what the future holds and it doesn't ease up because before you know it the children have arrived and now you are responsible for other people; it is no longer just about both of you and of course by now, the bills are piling up. Interestingly, God knows this and has made provision for us already. He has promised to always show us where to go, meaning we will never be stranded.

Interestingly, we can actually rely on this promise because we have seen Him keep this same promise to many others. Abraham for example; he also didn't know where he was headed, all he had was an instruction- *"Leave your own country behind you, and your own people, and go to the land I will guide you to. If you do, I will cause you to become the father of a great nation; I will bless you and make your name famous, and you will be a blessing to many others"* Genesis 12:1-2 (TLB). Something is striking here. In verse 2, it reveals that Abraham's being blessed was dependent on his obedience to God's instruction to leave his comfort zone and 'the familiar' and embark on a journey of uncertainties and to be clear, it was only uncertainty for Abraham.

God is committed to showing you like He showed Abraham how to be blessed and prosper even in the emptiest of places. We know that Abraham was blessed in all things including finances. This can be your story too; you too can be blessed.

SAY THIS TOGETHER

We declare that dry lands produce for us. We will dig wells in seasons of drought, and we will get water. Businesses and careers that have proven tough for others will work easily for us. We flourish where others dry up. Our case is different because we are led by the Spirit of God, we live full lives in Jesus Name. Amen.

FURTHER STUDY

Job 8:7 (HCSB), Isaiah 44:3 (NKJV) Genesis 12:1.

DAY NINE

Lasting Wealth

And I will make of you a great nation, and I will bless you [with abundant increase of favors] and make your name famous and distinguished, and you will be a blessing [dispensing good to others].

—Genesis 12: 2 [AMPC]

Before we go into today's devotion, I think it is important that we begin by establishing that even though the blessing includes financial prosperity, it is not limited to it. And this is important because I need you as a couple to look beyond financial increase to true and lasting wealth. As much as God wants you to be blessed, He also wants you to be a blessing to others. God also wants to bless us and give us a name with a lasting legacy.

Recently, I was on a trip to London and as I walked through Oxford Street, I got stopped by no less than six random people just to hear them say things like, "Thank you". "You have blessed me". "God has used you to save my marriage" and even though they gave me financial gifts and I left that place some thousand British pounds richer, it was the fact that I have been given the opportunity to add value to people's lives. Let's be honest, we all know that money answers to value; as long as you are giving people value, money will keep flowing to you.

I believe that God wants to bless us in such a way that it creates a money cycle; we bless people and they in turn bless us with an abundant increase of favours or money. God wants to give us the privilege of a family name that is famous and distinguished. A name that people respond to favourably. All we have to do is follow Him closely. The more we walk with Him, the more we can get clear instructions for our future and for the plans God has for us as a couple and as a family.

SAY THIS TOGETHER

[Insert your surname] is a great and distinguished name. As members of this family, we find favour wherever we go. We declare that kings, ministers, governors, and rulers seek us out to favour us. We declare that we are in positions to help people and we have the resources to make an impact in our society. In Jesus name. Amen.

FURTHER STUDY

Joshua 6:27 (ESV)

DAY TEN

Enjoy Your Labour

You will enjoy the fruit of your labour. How joyful and prosperous you will be!

—Psalm 128: 2 [NLT]

There's nothing more disheartening than working so hard and not enjoying the benefits of all the effort you put in. In fact, as a child of God, this is considered a curse because the covenant promises us that we will benefit from labour that isn't ours so how much more what we labour for?

Before you rush off and think this is just another fruit of your labour scripture, pay attention to what God is really saying to you here as a couple. God isn't just saying that you will eat the fruit of your labour, He is saying you will **enjoy** it. To enjoy means *to take delight or pleasure in something; to possess or benefit from something*. God wants you to find enjoyment in your work, life and marriage, by getting benefit out of it. It's so beautiful to see that even God is excited about how joyful, prosperous and happy we will be. That should tell you how good the fruit of your labour will be and how enjoyable it will be.

I also need to draw your attention to the fact that fruit also shows up sometimes at the end of a cycle; or seasonally. So this means that you will enjoy every season of your life together with wealth, prosperity, peace, health and everything you consider a fruit of labour.

SAY THIS TOGETHER

We declare that we will see the proceeds of our work, we will be alive and in health to enjoy it. We will not truncate the will of God for us with our own actions or inactions. It will never be said that we sowed, and birds came and ate up our seeds. We reap where we have invested, be it business, career, academics or people. We enjoy the

reward on earth, and we also enjoy the reward in heaven. In Jesus name. Amen.

FURTHER STUDY

Ecclesiastes 3:13 (ESV), Deuteronomy 12:7 (NIV).

DAY ELEVEN

A Rich Gift

May your land be blessed by the Lord with the precious gift of dew from the heavens and water from beneath the earth; with the rich fruit that grows in the sun, and the rich harvest produced each month; with the finest crops of the ancient mountains, and the abundance from the everlasting hills; with the best gifts of the earth and its bounty,

—Deuteronomy 33: 14-16 [NLT].

One of the things that I love about God is His intentionality. I love how detailed God is. See, if God says He is going to bless you, He never leaves you in doubt about what He intends to do. Just take a look at this scripture, blessings on your land, blessings from heaven, blessings from underneath the earth. He promises rich fruit; not ordinary or regular fruit but rich fruit meaning it is the best kind of result possible. He promises us a rich harvest produced each month; so you will earn income every month. You can expect to have results that have been stored up from things even your parents and those who have gone ahead of you have accrued and the abundance from the everlasting hills meaning it will be kind of blessings that you can leave as a legacy for your children and the best part is that it will be a gift.

The thing is, if you work for something, in itself it is noble, but there is something about a gift and the joy of getting it. God's blessing is a gift meaning that the result you get can never be commensurate with the effort you put in; it goes beyond your salary. In fact, there is such a thing as buying without money and it comes from embracing the grace that our Lord Jesus Christ has made available; the favour that comes with the grace and the abundant riches.

Come, buy your drinks, buy wine and milk. Buy without money – everything's free! Isaiah 55:1 (MSG).

God has been giving gifts from the beginning of time; the best gifts of the earth and its bounty. He's not about to stop now. He's promised to bless you, so pay attention to the gift that God has given you freely. Open your heart today to receive them.

SAY THIS TOGETHER

Favour comes to us from the east, west, north and south. Our minds are open to receive the precious gifts - the dew from the heavens and water from beneath the earth; the rich fruit that grows in the sun, and the rich harvest produced each month; the finest crops of the ancient mountains, and the abundance from the everlasting hills; the best gifts of the earth and its bounty. We attract free gifts. We declare that the funds, grants, sponsorship, and partnerships needed for our businesses, career goals and projects come to us when we need them and as much as we need them even to overflow in Jesus name. Amen.

FURTHER STUDY

Deuteronomy 28:8 (NKJV), Isaiah 55:1 (ERV)

DAY TWELVE

No More Hand-Me-Downs!

Powerful kings and mighty nations will satisfy your every need, as though you were a child nursing at the breast of a queen. You will know at last that I, the Lord, am your Savior and your Redeemer, the Mighty One of Israel.

—Isaiah 60:16 (NLT)

I'll give you only the best—no more hand-me-downs! Gold instead of bronze, silver instead of iron, bronze instead of wood, iron instead of stones.

—Isaiah 60:17(MSG}

If you've never had to wear hand-me-downs you just may not fully understand today's devotion. As the youngest of five boys, I definitely could not escape wearing hand-me-downs and after wearing clothes and shoes that have been handed down from four brothers, I understand when God says He wants to give you the best - brand new blessings.

The kind of wealth and blessings that God wants you to have will be the kind facilitated by kings of industries and it will be one that is globally relevant. I know sometimes it's hard to imagine every need you have fully met but God paints a very vivid picture for us. See yourself being nursed by a queen; meaning you will have someone who is able to satisfy your every need beyond your wildest dreams at your beck and call. Mothers usually pull all stops to ensure their children are satisfied even if they have to borrow or beg, now imagine having a mother who has it all. You will literally be living in the lap of luxury. That's why He promises us the best. You won't have to make do with crumbs, He's promising us the very best.

Are you aware of all God's promises to you as husband and wife? Are you aware of what has been prophesied about you? Are you allowing hand-me-downs because of your current location, position or situation? God says just like a nursing queen, He is giving you the best, so don't accept anything less. Out with the mediocre and give way to the premium.

SAY THIS TOGETHER

We thank you, Father, for you have prepared for us the choicest of the lot - we get the best deals, the best staff, the best bosses, the best offers, the best investors, and the best business partners. Anything we seek to move our work forward is available and we get the best. We do not settle for less than the best, we do not settle for what's available but what's preferable. We declare that our eyes are open to see what you have reserved for us as a couple. In Jesus name. Amen.

FURTHER STUDY

Genesis 45:18 (AMP).

DAY THIRTEEN

Transgenerational Wealth

The Lord shall increase you more and more,
you and your children

—Psalm 115 :14 [KJV]

God is such a trans-generational God. He doesn't just deal with individuals, He acts across multiple generations. So God wants to bless you, yes, but more importantly, He wants to bless you across generations; meaning your children, grandchildren, great grandchildren, down to your great, great, great, great, great, great, great, great, great, great, great, great .... *(I'm sure you get the picture)* grandchildren will be wealthy. God wants to start the blessing with you and your partner but He wants it to cascade down to many generations after you.

When we didn't have any children for the first couple of years in our marriage, I didn't really understand how important this promise was but once my daughter Hadassah arrived and her sister and brother followed soon after, I knew that I wanted them to have the best and not ever think of regressing. I wanted them to have much more than we ever did and thankfully, God wanted that too and being the loving God that He is, He has already made provision for that.

God's desire is to bless you with wealth as a couple which means you'll enjoy riches and your children will enjoy these riches in even greater proportions. I need your mind to grasp this; we are no longer just talking about your children's needs being sufficiently met, but that your generations after you will never lack. We are talking about trans-generational wealth.

SAY THIS TOGETHER

We declare that our children are blessed. They live beyond their needs being met because they are children of the promise. Our wealth transcends generations because of the covenant God made to our father, Abraham. We enjoy generational wealth in Jesus name. Amen.

FURTHER STUDY

Genesis 26:4 (NASB 1977), Genesis 13:16 (NLT).

DAY FOURTEEN

Abundant Grace

And God is able to make all grace [every favour and earthly blessing] come in abundance to you, so that you may always [under all circumstances, regardless of the need] have complete sufficiency in everything [being completely self-sufficient in Him] and have an abundance for every good work and act of charity.

—2 Corinthians 9:8 [AMP].

Because Pastor K and I are in ministry full time, we are always looking for ways to be a blessing to people which means we are either always planning a program, a seminar or an outreach, or paying someone's school fees or another's hospital bill. We are always coming up with what the Bible calls *'a good work or a charitable donation'*. What this means is that we always need money for one thing or the other and to be honest that used to put a strain on our finances because we were always at just barely enough…well, until we encountered this scripture. And, to be honest this was an encounter we had because it changed something for us.

I realised that God's word was clear on His ability to make **all grace** (every favour and earthly blessing) available; so whether we needed money or a favour it was available not one or the other and his promise was that it would **come in abundance,** so that we may **always under all circumstances**, **regardless of the need**, have **complete sufficiency** in **everything** completely self-sufficient in Him and have an **abundance** for **every good work** and act of charity. You need to look very closely at the highlighted words - abundance everywhere! *Hallelujah!*

I love how extravagant God is. Whether the need is for us or for blessing others, it is available in abundance. God doesn't do just enough, He is known for going overboard for His own and you and your spouse can be sure He will meet you at every point of your need. Ever since we saw this we have never had to beg or borrow for our personal lives, ministry, any good work or charitable donation. Isn't God good?

SAY THIS TOGETHER

We have an abundance mindset. We decree that we are never stranded. We decree that we have more than enough to meet all our personal needs and the good deeds we want to bless others with. We have enough to give for every charitable deed.

FURTHER STUDY

Joel 2:26 (AMP), Deuteronomy 28:11 (KJV).

DAY FIFTEEN

The Wait is Over

Yes indeed, it won't be long now." God's Decree. "Things are going to happen so fast your head will swim, one thing fast on the heels of the other. You won't be able to keep up. Everything will be happening at once—and everywhere you look, blessings! Blessings like wine pouring off the mountains and hills. I'll make everything right again for my people Israel

—Amos 9: 13-14 [MSG]

Have you ever had to wait an indefinite period for something? Are you currently waiting on God for a financial breakthrough? It gets really frustrating on that waiting line sometimes doesn't it? I know what it's like to be there because we have been there many times; waiting for God to show up at the eleventh hour and almost giving up hope yet still standing strong in faith.

Today, I'm here with some good news. God is saying that your wait is over. Things are going to change, and they will happen in such quick successions that it will blow your mind. One thing happening fast on the heels of the other. Just when you are sharing the testimony of a new job, there will be a promotion. Just when you are sharing that testimony, there will be a new car, then a new house, then multiple streams of income. There will be testimony after testimony. I know this because this is the story of our finances. This is why I'm sure God will do it for you because He is no respecter of persons; if He changed our story, He is bound to do it for you too. Just believe!

Another thing you must understand about God is His consistency, God doesn't start a thing and leave it halfway. He is a finisher. If He started blessing you as a couple, He has to continue. The wait is over, your breakthrough is here, and it is NOW!! Believe me, it will be a consistent outpour. Everywhere you look blessings pouring like wine. No half measures, no off days. With God, when it rains, it pours and when it pours, it doesn't pour water it pours wine.

SAY THIS TOGETHER

We declare that we experience no off days with inflow of finances, not just with us but with all those connected to us. We declare that every financial delay is broken in Jesus name. Thank you Father because resources come to us and they come in quick successions. Blessings everywhere we look in Jesus name.

FURTHER STUDY

Joel 3:18 (GNT)

DAY SIXTEEN

Willing and Able

You give them food when they need it. Ready to help, you open your hand. You give to every living thing the good things that they want."

—Psalms 145:15-16 [EASY]

I've heard people teach over and over again that God doesn't give you what you want; He gives you what you need. Well, I don't necessarily agree with that. I believe that God gives you what you need but He also gives you what you want. Today's scripture shows us the nature of God; He is not limited in resources; He gives both our wants and needs. He is a generous God; always willing to help.

Let us establish something here. God is not a man. He does not dispense help to His children according to their actions; that is more like what a man would do. Help is not a function of how much the recipient deserves it, but the benevolence of the giver. And we know by now that we serve a rich and benevolent God who gives without finding fault. When Adam needed help, God gave him a wife (Eve). When Adam and Eve sinned and lost everything, they were naked, ashamed and possibly cold. What did God do? He still helped them. Covered their cold, naked and ashamed bodies. Note, He was very displeased with them for their actions, but He couldn't deny Himself even in that situation. He is good and merciful and always ready and willing to help.

So, don't let the devil lie to you that your financial situation is as a result of God being displeased with you. God is not petty. Repent from that way of thinking and approach the throne of grace so that you might obtain mercy.

Remember, God is always willing and ready to help you.

SAY THIS TOGETHER

We come to you today knowing that you are a loving Father and that nothing can separate us from your Love. Help us know your love Lord and walk in that knowledge. The devil and his schemes have no hold over our minds in Jesus name. We are loved and helped by You.

FURTHER STUDY

Romans 8:18 (NLT), Psalm 121:1 (NIV)

DAY SEVENTEEN

Open Gates

Your gates will stay wide open around the clock to receive the wealth of many lands. The kings of the world will cater to you.

—Isaiah 60:11 [TLB]

No matter how much water you have in a tank until you turn the tap on, you will be left without water. The tap is the gate and it is the only thing standing between you and getting the water you need. A gate keeps from coming in and also keeps from going out. In this case, God is the source and the wealth gates include your jobs, businesses, relationships and so on. The word for today says that these gates will stay wide open round the clock. So we are not dealing with a pendulum kind of prosperity where it's up today and down tomorrow, but a consistent inflow of wealth from everywhere.

Our text for today also says "gates" which speaks of plural. You will enjoy multiple sources of income, with dignitaries making up your clientele base and money coming in different currencies. God is rich in every currency. He declares that the silver and the gold is His and that the cattle on a thousand hills is also His. he has no need to withhold it from you ever. He's a generous God who wants you to be blessed continually. His desire for you is that you will have wealth continually pouring into your family. He wants you to experience His generosity through different channels and multiple gates. So align with him by expecting it, believing in it and receiving it. Get ready for a continuous explosion of wealth. Your gates are open!

SAY THIS TOGETHER

We declare that our financial gates are open to us in every season of our lives. We declare that any deal we set out to close is closed. We command the king of industries to seek for us. Our clients are influential and high paying clients. Rulers and Kings seek out our products and our services. They travel from far to pay for them. Our businesses and jobs are attractive to foreign investors in Jesus name. Amen.

FURTHER STUDY

Isaiah 66:12 (CEV)

DAY EIGHTEEN

Dream Freely

He who did not withhold or spare [even] His own Son but gave Him up for us all, will He not also with Him freely and graciously give us all [other] things?"

—Romans 8:32 [AMPC]

Sometimes we need to be reminded of the God we are dealing with. I think we tend to limit Him because we measure His abilities with the same metrics that we use to measure the abilities of men. But it is important to know that God is not intimidated by your needs, desires or requests. He is more than capable- He is able and willing. He has already given you His only begotten son Jesus, so what could He possibly hold back from you?

Understanding this truly changed our finances. Coming to the realization that there was nothing that God was not willing to give us made us begin to dream a lot more concerning our finances. I remember us having many crazy conversations and agreeing on specific amounts in specific currencies. Calling forth money by name and even though at the time it sounded and felt crazy because our bank balance didn't seem to balance at all, we kept at it reminding ourselves that God had already given us the most difficult thing to give - His son. So what was a few million dollars? Today, it feels like a dream because not only has God met our expectations, He has exceeded them.

It is rather belittling to God when His children keep adjusting their dreams in fear that it would be too much for God to do. If only you know who your Father is. This is a call to dream freely, make your request boldly to the Father, He is in no way limited. Whatever you both agree you want, He can and will make it happen.

SAY THIS TOGETHER

We decree that we are unlimited. Our hearts are open to receive all the good things You have in store for us. We prosper in every currency. Nothing good is withheld from us. We dream freely and wildly and we enjoy God's extravagance as we do. Nothing is impossible for God to give us or do for us.

FURTHER STUDY

Genesis 17:6 (NLT), 1 Timothy 6: 17 (NKJV).

DAY NINETEEN

The Same Measure

Give, and it will be given to you: good measure, pressed down, shaken together, and running over will be put into your bosom. For with the same measure that you use, it will be measured back to you."

—Luke 6: 38 [NKJV]

This is the scripture that changed my finances. The day I discovered it and got the revelation behind it, was the day I moved from barely enough to overflowing. We focus mostly on the first part of this scripture which says, *"Give, and it will be given to you: good measure, pressed down, shaken together, and running over will be put into your bosom."* Many times we ignore the latter part which is an upgrade of the first one- *"...for with the same measure that you use, it will be measured back to you."* Measure speaks of a standard of measurement. What this means is that you can determine the measure with which you receive by the measure with which you give. This was such a light bulb moment for me.

I came across this scripture when I was tired of operating in the thousand realm in my finances. I needed to break out into the million realm. It was at this point I knew what I had to do. I told my wife that we needed to start giving in millions to break into the million realm. Let me be honest with you, we didn't have a million naira. We were so far from having anything like that but we started to work towards it. We saved everything we got and sold gifts we received until we saved up one million naira. We made a lot of sacrifices and it took us quite some time to pull all our resources together to make up one million naira. Once we did, we sowed the entire sum. In less than six months, we had broken through the thousand barrier. It's been an easy flow of millions since then. In fact it worked so much that we decided to also do the same with respect to currency because we had come to understand that if you want naira you sow in naira so inevitably if you want dollars you sow in dollars. a simple revelation that turned our finances around; give using the measure you want to receive in. It's simple really.

Decide today as a couple what your measure should be then give with that measure so you can receive in the same measure.

SAY THIS TOGETHER

Father, we thank you for creating this principle that empowers us to determine the measure at which we receive based on our seed because our hearts are generous. We give cheerfully and consistently out of love for You, your kingdom and those in need as you direct us. Thank you for increasing our measures. We change levels financially as we give in accordance with your word.

FURTHER STUDY

2 Corinthians 9:6 (NLT)

DAY TWENTY

All-Around Good Life

God, your God, will outdo himself in making things go well for you: you'll have babies, get calves, grow crops, and enjoy an all-around good life. Yes, God will start enjoying you again, making things go well for you just as he enjoyed doing it for your ancestors.

—Deuteronomy 30:9 [MSG]

Are you coming from a place where you enjoyed riches and the bliss of it all to a current state that doesn't quite measure up? God is not a God of the 'good old days', with Him it is 'brighter and brighter unto the perfect day' (*Proverbs 4:18*). If you have found yourself in this position, God assures you that He will restore. He does take pleasure in His children's prosperity, especially those who worship Him with their wealth. So, if you think you enjoyed riches in the past, get ready, keep your arms open to receive because God is about to outdo Himself in your family.

Interestingly, God has given us a glimpse into the way He was with our ancestors - Abraham, Isaac, Jacob, David, Solomon, the list is inexhaustive. God takes great pleasure in spoiling us. In fact the generosity of God is something He enjoys. We are not in any way disturbing God when we expect the blessings of God. Don't expect Him to be tired of blessing you or giving to you. There has to be a mindset shift. This scripture tells us that God blessing us is enjoyment for Him; the more He blesses us the more He enjoys us again. This is such an uplifting thought; that I bring God pleasure when I am blessed. He loves to lavish me with blessings all round, whether it is material, emotional, spiritual or physical blessings, He wants us to have them because it brings Him joy.

As a couple God wants us to have everything we desire, babies, food, money, houses, healthy relationships and everything that brings us enjoyment. The beauty is that as we enjoy these all round blessings, He enjoys giving them to us too.

SAY THIS TOGETHER

We declare and believe that the wealth that we once enjoyed is nothing compared to the riches that are coming to us. We enjoy the good things of life. We constantly bask in the lavish extravagance of our Father in heaven. We are rich in human and non-human resources more than we have ever been. We declare that all goes well with us in Jesus name.

FURTHER STUDY

Jeremiah 32:41 (BSB), Ecclesiastes 5:19 (ESV)

DAY TWENTY ONE

New Wine

"Then the Lord will be careful for his land. He will be kind to his people. He will answer them and he will say, 'I am giving you new wine and food and oil. You will have enough to fill you up. I will never again let people in other countries laugh about you."

—Joel 2:18-19 [EASY]

In the times we live in, the most respected "person" in any gathering is money. Do you know why? It is because money must agree to every plan, agenda or project for it to happen. Guess who the second most respected person in every gathering is? The person who has the money. I would really like to say this is not true, but it is. To be fair, it may not be Ideal, but it is what is obtainable or like the popular saying, "it is what it is!"

Just look around you today, the richest member of most families who is generous with his money is given a degree of respect and honour above others, while the poorest or not-so-rich gets some disdain with every statement he makes or every idea he brings. (*Proverbs 14:20, Proverbs 19:4*). To be scorned because of poverty is not definitely not God's will for you as a couple. Sadly whether we like it or not in the world we live in today, nobody wants to be associated with a 'nobody'.

Don't be deceived, poverty is not God's will for His children. It is God's desire that in every gathering you are given the front seat because of your generosity *(3 John 1:*2), as He also trusts that the platform would be used as an opportunity to draw men to Him and to worship Him. (*Proverbs 3:9*). So as as couple agree that God will give you new wine and create for you both a sweetness and a relevance in your extended families and communities and sphere of influence.

SAY THIS TOGETHER

We declare that we are Blessed in every currency. We will not be laughed at or scorned because of a lack of money. We have more than enough to contribute to every good cause. We lend to nations and borrow from none. Thank You Lord for we are self-sufficient and require no aid or support because we are furnished in abundance for every good work and charitable donation. Thank you for overflowing wealth is ours in Jesus name. Amen.

FURTHER STUDY

Proverbs 14:20, Proverbs 19:4, Deuteronomy 11:11-12 (TLB)

DAY TWENTY TWO

Make Room for Increase

May the Lord, the God of your fathers increase you a thousand times more than you are, and bless you, just as He has promised you!

—Deuteronomy 1:11 [NASB}

One of the signs of blessing is increase. All over scripture when God talks about any one being blessed you would see that clearly increase is mentioned. Increase in the body, the mind, property, servants, relationships, money and other things that we classify as visible increase. It's no different with everyday life. Take for instance, if you run a business and you start to open new branches, that only means one thing: your customer base is growing wider, and one branch is not enough to cater to them.

Branching out is indicative of increase and that's indicative of more inflow of income. God's promise to Abraham that flows to us includes increase and multiplication. What you should be doing right now is making room by faith for the things that God has promised to do for you. Interestingly, the bible tells us that the God of our fathers will bring increase so what that means is that we would look at the life of our fathers, if there was increase in their lives then we should expect an increase too because God is the same yesterday, today and forever. He actually does not change. Also we are assured that His word does not fail. If He promised that as a couple you would have a good reward for your labour it means that by becoming a couple you are entitled to increase.

So what should you do now? Start planning to branch out, start planning to hire more staff, start planning to raise people who can represent you in the other branches. God won't give you what you are not prepared for because it might break you. God has promised increase and we know He watches over His word to fulfil it. Now the ball is in your court. Start to build capacity. Spread out because increase is coming.

SAY THIS TOGETHER

Heavenly Father, we thank you for where we are, but we are aware it is nothing close to the increase we are launching into. We thank you for expansion, growth, reach and impact. Thank you for multiple streams of income. We ask for wisdom and understanding on how to build capacity and make room for the increase.

FURTHER STUDY:

Deuteronomy 28 (NIV). Isaiah 54:1-2. Ecclesiastes 4:9. Proverbs 18:22.

DAY TWENTY THREE

A Luxurious Life

Yahweh is my best friend and my shepherd. I always have more than enough. He offers a resting place for me in his luxurious love. His tracks take me to an oasis of peace near the quiet brook of bliss.

—Psalm 23:1-2 [TPT]

A luxurious life is beyond just having money. Imagine waking up every morning to a life of bliss and a lot of pleasant surprises that are planned by God into your daily experiences. Now you have become rich and can afford many good things but God in His lavish goodness still chooses to bless you with a lot of goodies which is a result of His goodness. You now become used to being pampered and you enjoy a high quality of life filled with things money can buy and money cannot buy. This is exactly what Jesus meant in John 10:10b … *I came that they may have life, and have it in abundance [to the full, till it overflows].*

Luxury is not a sin. In fact, God wants you to enjoy the fine things of life. They are not reserved for the heathen; they are actually for the children of God. You are not being carnal when you desire luxury cars, mansions, earning money in every currency of the world, being a respected individual because God will also give you the influence to complement your affluence. It becomes a problem however when you make those desires replace your longing for righteousness and the kingdom of God.

As for luxury, God wants you to have and enjoy it. A good earthly father who has so much wealth derives joy in watching his children play with the toys He got them. These luxuries, you know, are like toys to God and it would give Him so much joy to watch you play around with them.

Relax and open your mind to luxury. It is God's desire for you.

SAY THIS TOGETHER

Thank you, Father, for always taking care of us. We declare that we never experience lack. Our hearts are open to the luxurious life you have prepared for us and we bask in it. We declare that we do not ever have to manage resources for fear of shortage, but we always have more than enough.

FURTHER STUDY:

1 Kings 10: 13-25 (ERV)

DAY TWENTY FOUR

God's Favour

And the LORD was with Joseph, and he became a successful man, serving in the household of his Egyptian master. When his master saw that the LORD was with him and made him prosper in all he did Joseph found favor in his sight and became his personal attendant. Potiphar put him in charge of his household and entrusted him with everything he owned.

—Genesis 39:2-4 [BSB]

As a couple one of the things you must never underestimate is the favour of God. In fact it would be a huge mistake to do so seeing as that is one of the major things the Bible tells us to expect to experience. Once you find a wife the bible says that what should ordinarily follow is favour. One of the things you must reflect on is how powerful favour is and how it can alter a person's life. Now imagine combined favour as a couple and the effects it will have on your finances.

Regardless of what position you are in your business or career, if you have the favour of God in your life, you'll stand out. Take a look at Joseph who came into Egypt as a slave but that didn't matter in fact, it was barely talked about. The Bible calls him blessed and favoured and prosperous. Can you imagine that? A slave? Yes but a favoured slave. That's what kept moving him up the ranks. Even when he was accused falsely and imprisoned, he prospered. A prosperous prisoner, imagine that. His position was not the reason for his prosperity but because God was with him. He was favoured by God.

Why was he the most loved son of his father? He was neither the oldest, the strongest, nor the youngest. He was simply favoured by God. God's blessing is no respecter of official position or status. To enjoy this benefit, simply be conscious of the blessing and let that consciousness rule your attitude. As a family, be conscious of the favour of God that you carry and activate it by faith daily and watch God move you into realms of prosperity you never thought possible.

SAY THIS TOGETHER

Thank you Father for your mighty hand that is constantly upon us, our businesses and careers. Thank you for the position where we currently occupy. We believe that you are with us and for that reason, we find favour with those who matter in our industries. Thank you for your promotion. We pray that our steps are continually ordered by you as we climb up great heights in our careers and businesses in Jesus name. Amen.

FURTHER STUDY:

Psalm 75: 6-7 (NLT).

DAY TWENTY FIVE

Don't Worry

And don't worry about food—what to eat and drink; don't worry at all that God will provide it for you. All mankind scratches for its daily bread, but your heavenly Father knows your needs. He will always give you all you need from day to day if you will make the Kingdom of God your primary concern.

—Luke 12: 29-31 [TLB]

Worrying about provision is an indirect way of telling God that you don't trust that He is willing and able to provide for and take care of you like He said He would, making Him out to be a liar and that is an insult to His person.

As it is written, *People who "worry their prayers" are like wind-whipped waves. Don't think you're going to get anything from the Master that way. James 1:7 (MSG)*

Sometimes it looks as though worrying is an inevitable state of the human mind, I mean, take a look at all that is happening around the world, especially economically. We are constantly thrown into different recessions. Your mind begins to tell you that the natural thing to do is to begin to worry and panic but that's a lie of the devil. Listen, everything happening has already been anticipated by God and an antidote has been given; *Don't worry about anything; instead, pray about everything; tell God your needs, and don't forget to thank him for his answers. Philippians 4:6 (TLB).*

There is only one attitude that gets an answer from God and that is the attitude of faith, and worry which is an offshoot of fear is the exact opposite. Worrying about money never makes money come, it rather shifts you farther away from the position where you can receive from God. worry must never be your disposition to any situation - financial or otherwise.

SAY THIS TOGETHER

We do not operate from a place of fear because we trust that You, Father, are aware of our desires. You are willing and You are able. We receive the provision that has been made for us. We thank You for all our needs are met and all our bills are paid. Worry has no place in this family because we are in absolute faith that the lord is our shepherd therefore we have all that we need and more than enough.

FURTHER STUDY

James 1:7 (MSG), Matthew 7:7, Philippians 4:6 (AMP),

DAY TWENTY SIX

Divine Timing

The king was talking with Gehazi, servant to the Holy Man, saying, "Tell me some stories of the great things Elisha did." It so happened that as he was telling the king the story of the dead person brought back to life, the woman whose son was brought to life showed up asking for her home and farm. Gehazi said, "My master the king, this is the woman! And this is her son whom Elisha brought back to life!" The king wanted to know all about it, and so she told him the story. The king assigned an officer to take care of her, saying, "Make sure she gets everything back that's hers, plus all profits from the farm from the time she left until now."

—2 Kings 8:4-6 [MSG]

There are some blessings that come into your life based on a factor called the unforced rhythms of grace (which we can also refer to as divine coincidence). The Bible talks about the footsteps of the righteous being ordered by the Lord (Psalms 37:23). You and your spouse must believe God to order your steps into some divine arrangements like in the narrative in 2 kings chapter 8. The amazing thing about this story is that she could have come to the king at any time but she chose that exact moment when she was being discussed. I believe she was led by God at that exact time.

There are certain opportunities you may never know exist except the Lord leads you to them and that is why couples must always yield to the leading of the Holy Spirit. There are many stories of people who were led by the Holy Spirit to either go somewhere or make a call and it was perfect timing for a breakthrough or a desired harvest. So, you as a couple must be sensitive to the promptings of God in your life and act on them promptly. Just Imagine the Shunamite woman had delayed going to the King's palace, she would have missed a divine setup which led to having her land restored to her after seven years and because God is just such an extraordinary strategist, not only were her lands returned, she was also given the profits accrued within that time - No loss! Hallelujah!

This can be your story if you will yield to God's leading as a family. Even the things that seem like a disadvantage will become a divine setup to your advantage.

SAY THIS TOGETHER

Our steps are ordered by the Lord. We walk into opportunities and favour. We gain royal recognition. We declare that all that is due us, everything that has our name on them, everything that belongs to us is released and is accorded to us. Every benefit that we have been denied is restored to us with compensation. Every financial loss we have ever encountered is turned around for our gain in Jesus name. Amen.

FURTHER STUDY

Psalm 37: 23 (NIV)

DAY TWENTY SEVEN

Our Covenant

It is a waste of time to get up early and stay up late, trying to make a living. The Lord provides for those he loves, even while they are sleeping.

—Psalm 127:2 [ERV]

THE HUSTLE IS REAL!" If you haven't said those words before, I'm sure you've heard them said by someone you know. Well, let's settle this once for all that as a couple those words or any other phrase that validates hustle will no longer be mentioned in your life or home. The funny thing is that many people pride themselves on the fact that they hustle meanwhile as a Christian you must understand that the first time hustle was mentioned or implied in scripture was as a result of sin and the curse had taken effect on mankind. God's original plan was never for man to toil and hustle and labour before he could enjoy prosperity; all that came after the fall. So to pride yourself in a curse is ignorance.

However, Jesus came to change all that and restore us back to our original state which is that our blessings are not dependent on work. We don't work to eat, we work to be useful to God and humanity. Trying to do it all on your own is a waste of your time. Everytime you think you should wake up earlier or go to bed later, you're moving your eyes from God as your source to hustle as your source. The bible makes it clear that this is an attempt in futility. To truly understand this scripture let's look at it in the Contemporary English Version [CEV] ***Without the help of the LORD it is useless to build a home or to guard a city. It is useless to get up early and stay up late in order to earn a living. God takes care of his own, even while they sleep.*** Just look at that, God takes care of His own whether they hustle or not in fact the Bible says it's useless to do it. From today let your faith be in God and not in hustle.

SAY THIS TOGETHER

We thank you father for showing us your extravagant love. We thank you because life is easy for us. We do not subscribe to the hustle culture but we embrace your provision and favour. We declare that the hustle life is not our portion because even in our sleep we are provided for as a family therefore we will not wake up early and go to bed late running around trying to earn a living

FURTHER STUDY

Psalm 3:5 (NIV), Proverbs 10:22 (NIV).

DAY TWENTY EIGHT

The Blessing

The blessing of the Lord brings wealth,
without painful toil for it.

—Proverbs 10:22 [NIV]

It has become customary practice to attach nobility to toiling. But remember like we stated yesterday that painful toiling is one of the consequences of Adam's disobedience.

" And to Adam, God said, "Because you listened to your wife and ate the fruit when I told you not to, I have placed a curse upon the soil. All your life you will struggle to extract a living from it ". Genesis 3:17 (TLB).

It was upon this curse that the 'painful toil' culture was established. These days we call it 'hustling' and 'grinding'. But we have been redeemed from the curse, we are children of obedience and descendants of the blessing. (Deuteronomy 28). As long as you are walking in obedience to God's commands, you do not have to toil day and night, you do not have to compromise your values, you do not have to sweat, struggle or beg to get the wealth that has already been allocated to you. It has your name on it, so walk in with an owner's confidence and take it.

The thing about the blessing of God is that it makes; yes, it has the ability to make you whatever God has commanded it to make you and in this case if you read the king james version of proverbs 10:22, you will see that it is commanded to make you rich and rich without painful toil and without added sorrow.

SAY THIS TOGETHER

We do not believe in hustle culture. We declare that wealth comes to us with ease. We do not struggle for money. We do not lobby for favours. We do not compromise our values for riches. We are carried on the winds of God's blessings in Jesus name. Amen.

FURTHER STUDY

1 Peter 5:7 (NKJV), Matthew 6:27 (AMP).

DAY TWENTY NINE

An End to Toiling

You know the grace of our Lord Jesus Christ. You know that he gave up his heavenly riches for you. He gave up everything so that you could be richly blessed.

—2 Corinthians 8:9 [ERV]

Understanding the riches Jesus gave in exchange for your poverty is key to walking in prosperity. He owned everything, the gold and the silver, but took up your nothing and gave you his everything and said all you had to do is accept that He did that. This knowledge changes your mindset and attitude towards riches and wealth. You begin to understand the benefit of all that Jesus did for you on the cross.

Sadly a lot of times we don't fully grasp what Jesus did for us and we can often let it go to waste. What Jesus achieved for you during His time here on earth and by his death is something that is unquantifiable. Do you know that, as long as you have believed in the finished works of Christ, it is impossible for you to be poor? That version of you died and was buried over 2000 years ago. The only version of you that exists is rich and richly blessed. So you have to start walking and talking like one who is rich because you are.

Also, it is important that you don't cower in the face of money, only poor people do that. Regardless of what it might currently look like physically, it doesn't change who you truly are- you are Rich. As a couple, you must take time daily to remind yourselves of the wealth that you have received in Christ Jesus. Encourage each other to dream freely and live fully aware of all that Christ has done for you, expecting wealth and riches to be your reality .

SAY THIS TOGETHER

Poverty was nailed to the cross and buried over 2000 years ago, therefore, it has no place in this family today. We are richly blessed in all currencies and our riches are of the heavenly kind. Therefore, they cannot be affected by earthly elements.

FURTHER STUDY

Proverbs 8:21 (CEV).

DAY THIRTY

The Power of Tithing

Bring all the tithes into the storehouse, That there may be food in My house, And try Me now in this," says the Lord of hosts, "If I will not open for you the windows of heaven and pour out for you such blessing that there will not be room enough to receive it. "And I will rebuke the devourer for your sakes, so that he will not destroy the fruit of your ground, nor shall the vine fail to bear fruit for you in the field," says the Lord of hosts; "And all nations will call you blessed, For you will be a delightful land," Says the Lord of hosts.

—Malachi 3:10-12 [NKJV]

There have been arguments over the years about the principle of tithing but today is not the day to delve into that. I am just going to ask two questions:

1. Are you a faithful tither?

2. If yes, do you know the benefits you are entitled to as a faithful tither?

Here's an old trick in the devil's playbook. He is aware of what lies on the other side of obedience, so he steps right in and presents logical reasons why you should disobey instructions or disregard principles, with the hope that you would bite. For him (satan) it is conquest. He did it with the first Adam, through Eve. They bit and lost the garden, their dominion, and the most important relationship there was. (*Genesis 3).*

Satan tried it again with the second Adam, *Matthew 4: 1-11* but of course, he lost and Jesus gained everything. Interestingly, he is still at it. Trying to sell 'common sense' to the children of God in exchange for their inheritance. Are you going to bite or are you going to focus on obeying the word of God? Today as a couple commit to complete obedience.

SAY THIS TOGETHER.

We declare that we have an affinity for good things. We attract good things. Good things come to us. Because we are faithful tithers, the devourer in the name of sickness, loss or bad investment does not come near our dwelling. We declare that heaven is open unto us and we receive the rain of blessings that is due tithers.

FURTHER STUDY

Leviticus 27:30 (AMP), Proverbs 3:9 (NLT).

DAY THIRTY ONE

No Limits

And my God will liberally supply (fill until full) your every need according to His riches in glory in Christ Jesus.

—Philippians 4:19 [AMP]

Budgeting is a long known practice that teaches financial discipline. A proper practice, if I must say, to plan around your earnings. It is even scriptural to 'count the cost' before embarking on a project. Then we also hear good quotes like, "Cut your coat according to your cloth". This is founded on really good motives, but we should be careful that we don't lose touch of the abundant riches of God by creating limits in our minds from our knowledge of economics, or its fear thereof.

"The earth and everything on it belong to the Lord" – Psalm 24:1

Everything includes everything.

As bad as you are, you still know how to give good gifts to your children. But your heavenly Father is even more ready to give good things to people who ask. – Matthew 7:11 (CEV).

Don't limit your asking, dreaming or planning to your earthly knowledge of economics. Your supply is from a heavenly realm of abundance and overflow and God is never intimidated by your requests. Be careful not to limit God like the Israelites did many years ago and by doing so did not get the full benefits of walking with God. God's instruction is to "open your mouth wide and i will fill it." As a couple, make up your mind today that you will never go back to a place of lack or poverty but that as a couple you would walk in the fullness of all that Jesus has given you and is willing to give to you and your family.

SAY THIS TOGETHER.

We declare that the economic situation of this world does not determine our supply. Our wealth is not affected by our environment. We acknowledge that You are able and willing to meet every need we have. Our eyes are fixed on Your abundant riches and not on the news or the stock market. We live above the systems of this world. We enjoy unlimited supplies all the days of our lives in Jesus name. Amen!

FURTHER STUDY

Matthew 7: 9-11 (ERV). Psalm 24:1 (KJV)

REFERENCE

Institute for Divorce financial Analysts(IDFA), (2023),https://institutedfa.com/leading-causes-divorce/#:~:text=According%20to%20a%20 recent%20survey,money%20issues%22%20 (22%25).

ABOUT THE AUTHORS

Mildred and Kingsley Okonkwo are specialists when it comes to making marriage work. They are the Lead Coaches at Love, Dating and Marriage Ministry (@ldmwithpk); one of the foremost marriage and relationship ministries to ever come out of Africa. They are also the hosts of Together Forever Conference, an annual conference for married couples to re-ignite their love which has recorded many testimonies of restored marriages.

Having taught on relationships for well over two decades, Mildred and Kingsley have authored several books and spoken at countless conferences and seminars across continents. They have been a blessing to thousands of marriages. They believe that with the right knowledge, everyone can have the marriage of their dreams!

They are also the lead pastors at David's Christian Centre, a faith-based ministry located in Lagos, Nigeria. They are blessed with two adorable daughters and one amazing son.

Made in the USA
Columbia, SC
23 April 2025